The Collected Poems
of
John Galsworthy

The Collected Poems
of
John Galsworthy

New York

Charles Scribner's Sons

1934

CONTENTS

IN WAR TIME

THE SUN, THE MOON, THE ENDLESS DREAM

DEDICATION

Thine is the solitude that rare flowers know,
Whose beauty holds the charm of secrecy.
Of all the flowers that in the garden grow,
None other has thy sweet supremacy.
For thine's the oldest secret in the world:
How to be loved, and still to keep apart —
Flower full blown, and bud not yet unfurled —
Gold-fortuned I, whose very breath thou art!

ERRANTRY

COME ! Let us lay a lance in rest,
And tilt at windmills under a wild sky !
For who would live so petty and unblest
That dare not tilt at something ere he die;
Rather than, screened by safe majority,
Preserve his little life to little end,
And never raise a rebel cry !

Ah! for a weapon so sublime,
That, lifted, counts no cost of woe or weal,
Since Fate demands it shivered every time !
When in the wildness of our charge we reel
Men laugh indeed—the sweeter heavens smile,
For all the world of fat prosperity
Can not outweigh that broken steel !

The echo of our challenging
Sets swinging all the bells of ribaldry,
And yet those other hidden bells that ring
The faint and wondering chimes of sympathy
Within the true cathedral of our souls—
So, crystal-clear, the shepherd's pipe will move
His browsing flock to reverie.

1

God save the pennon, in the morn,
That signals moon to stand, and sun to fly;
That flutters when the weak is overborne
To stem the tide of fate and certainty.
It knows not reason, and it seeks no fame,
But has engraven round its stubborn wood:
"Knight-errant to Eternity!"

So! Undismayed beneath the clouds
Shall float the banner of forlorn defence—
A jest to the complacency of crowds,
But haloed with the one diviner sense:
To hold itself as nothing to itself;
And in the quest of the imagined star
To lose all thought of recompense!

COURAGE

COURAGE is but a word, and yet, of words,
The only sentinel of permanence;
The ruddy watch-fire of cold winter days,
We steal its comfort, lift our weary swords,
And on. For faith—without it—has no sense;
And love to wind of doubt and tremor sways;
And life for ever quaking marsh must tread.

Laws give it not; before it prayer will blush;
Hope has it not; nor pride of being true;
'Tis the mysterious soul which never yields,
But hales us on to breast the rush
Of all the fortunes we shall happen thro';
And when Death calls across his shadowy fields—
Dying, it answers: "Here ! I am not dead !"

TRUE DEEDS

THERE is a Lantern of true, silent deeds
Swinging refulgent in the spacious air,
Where restless words, those misty messengers
Sob out their subtle hearts with yea and nay,
And, like to myriad insects fluttering,
Brush with their wings that spiring crystal horn
That keeps inviolate a constant light.

'Tis the presiding sun at every birth,
The soft consoling moon at every death;
And in the middle watches of our life
What is it but the one sweet single star,
Whose twinkle, like the laughter of dear thoughts,
Upon the feeble vadings of our hearts
Sheds ever rays of tender irony!

Come night, come day! It knows no faltering,
Swung o'er the hubbub of a windy world.
No victory, but it doth halo round,
No sad defeat, whose wounds it hath not bathed;
And in those trackless wilds where nothing's done—
A mournful eye, its faint far glimmering
Peers through the distance everlastingly.

4

LOVE

Love !—that love which comes so stealthily,
And takes us up, and twists us as it will—
What fever'd hours of agony 'twill bring !
How oft we wake and cry: "God set me free
Of love—to never love again !" And still
We fall, and clutch it by the knees, and cling
And press our lips—and so, once more are glad !

And if it go, or if it never come,
Through what a grieving wilderness of pain
We travel on ! In prisons stripped of light
We blindly grope, and wander without home.
The friendless winds that sweep across the plain—
The beggars meeting us at silent night—
Than we, are not more desolate and sad !

LOVE

(Earlier Version)

LIKE lights that pass, each motion of the mind
Flies through the world, seeking its fellow thought;
And if but in the twinkling of his days
A man shall chance to meet the kindred one—
Then happiness ! No more he needs to burn
Beside the fire of dearth that pipe, whose smoke
Prays to the heedless stars of lonely men.

Then in a rare and wonderful abode
Where wit comes not, and thinking has no part,
A tender comedy is played and played,
That holds the magic meaning of the spheres,
And, than the murmur of two meeting rills
Has no more sense—yet—all the sense there is
In this, our dream, and that, our coming sleep.

And when it's gone, or if it never come,
Then in the grieving dark we grope along;
Within the shuttered mazes of our souls
We wander, and again fall wandering.
The endless winds that sweep across the plain,
Beggars who meet us in the silent night,
Are not more shorn of company than we !

6

BEAUTY

BEAUTY is not a set and flawless rule;
She spells the mist, and with a silver wing
Hovers upon the shades of grey and brown
No less than on a rich embroidery.
She is a kind of rhythm, an accord
Of dreaming notes, so vague and mystical
That on a breath irrelevant, they fade.

She subtly whispers her imaginings,
And hath a tender breath more delicate
Than far-blown scent of gorse on distant hills.
If we but catch the glimmer of her wing,
Then witchery ! We needs must follow her ! . . .
If never on our path she comes along—
Then are we lost, for always we are blind.

The phantasy of yearning, and of hope,
She comes to naught in Comprehension's grasp;
No feather balanced on the Southern gale
Is more impalpable than Beauty's face.
We shall pursue her till our days are out;
If e'er she vanish, Life is spent—'tis time
To draw the curtain for a last goodnight !

ACCEPTATION

Blue sky, grey stones, and the far sea,
The lark's song, trilling over me;
Grey stones, blue sky, and the green weed—
You have no sense that I can read;
Nor on the wind's breath passing by
Comes any meaning melody!
Blue sky, grey stones, and the far sea,
Lark's song, green weed, wind melody—
You are! And must accepted be!

SERENITY

The smiling sea
And dunes and sky
Dream; and the bee
Goes dreaming by.

In heaven's field
Moon's scimitar
Is drawn to shield
One dreaming star.

The dreaming flowers
And lovers nod.
Serene these hours—
Serene is God.

REMINDER

Each star to rise and shine and fade—
Each bird that sings its song and sleeps—
Each spark of spirit fire that leaps
Within me—of One Flame are made!

THE SEEDS OF LIGHT

Once of a mazy afternoon, beside that southern sea,
I watched a shoal of sunny beams come swimming
    close to me.
Each was a whited candle-flamelet, flickering in air;
Each was a silver daffodil astonied to be there;
Each was a diving summer star, its brightness come
    to lave;
And each a little naked spirit leaping on the wave.

And while I sat, and while I dreamed, beside that
    summer sea,
There came the fairest thought of all that ever came
    to me;
The tiny lives of tiny men, no more they seemed to
    mean
Than one of those sweet seeds of light sown on that
    water green;
No more they seemed, no less they seemed, than shim-
    merings of sky—
The little sunny smiles of God that glisten forth and
    die.

DEVON AND OTHER SONGS
FOR MUSIC

GAULZERY (GALSWORTHY) MOOR

Moor of my name, where the road leads high,
Thro' heather and bracken, gorse and grass,
Up to the crown of the western sky,
A questing traveller, slow, I pass.
Silent and lonely the darkening moor,
The beasts are bedded, the birds are gone,
Never a farm, nor a cottage door,
And I on the road alone—alone;
And the south-west wind is beginning to croon
And a listening lonely pine-tree sways;
And behind it is hanging a golden moon
For a resting sign at the cornerways.
    A thousand years since the stranger came,
    And homed him here, and gave me name.

LAND SONG OF THE WEST COUNTRY

The lanes are long, and 'ome is far,
But we'll go joggin', joggin' on.
Up dimsy sky, 'ere comes a star,
Over the bank the flowers peep
To see if 'tis the time to sleep.
But we'll go joggin' on.

The sunset's sinkin' down apace,
But we'll go joggin', joggin' on.
The land's all like a maiden's face,
The more yu look the less yu see,
'Tis all a movin' mystery.
And we'll go joggin' on.

The trout are risin' in the stream,
We ford it, joggin', joggin' on.
The mill-wheel's turnin' in a dream;
The chafer's boomin' over'ead,
And every liddl' bird's in bed.
And we go joggin' on.

The cottages are prayin' smoke,
As we go joggin', joggin' on.
The 'ayrick's bonneted a-poke;
The beasts are chewin' at their ease
The evenin' cud beneath the trees,
As we go joggin' on.

There's many a teasin' drop o' rain
As we go joggin', joggin' on;
And many a brave while fine again;
There's many a dip and many a rise,
And many a smile o' dinky eyes.
There's many a scent, and many a tune,
And over all the liddl' müne,
As we go joggin' on!

VILLAGE SLEEP SONG

SLEEP ! all who toil;
No longer creaks the harvest wain,
For sleeping lies the harvest day,
Asleep the winding leafy lane
Where none's afoot to miss his way.

Sleep ! village street,
You've stared too long upon the sun;
Now turn you to the gentle moon.
Sleep ! windows—for your work is done;
Tomorrow's light will come too soon !

Sleep ! Sleep ! The heat
Is over, in the darkened house.
A night-jar's spinning in the brake
And—hark !—the floating owls have come
To try and keep the hours awake.

Sleep ! honey hives !
And swallow's flight and thrushes' call !
Sleep, tongues, a little, while you may,
And let night's cool oblivion fall
On all the gossip of the day.

Sleep! Men and wives,
A sweetness of refreshment steal;
The morning star can vigil keep;
Too quickly turns the slumber wheel!—
And all you little children, sleep!

DEVON TO ME!

Where my fathers stood
Watching the sea,
Gale-spent herring boats
Hugging the lea;
There my Mother lives,
Moorland and tree.
Sight o' the blossom!
Devon to me!

Where my fathers walked,
Driving the plough;
Whistled their hearts out—
Who whistles now?
There my Mother burns
Fire faggots free.
Scent o' the wood-smoke!
Devon to me!

Where my fathers sleep,
Turning to dust,
This old body throw
When die I must !
There my Mother calls,
Wakeful is She !
Sound o' the west-wind !
Devon to me !

Where my fathers lie,
When I am gone,
Who need pity me
Dead? Never one !
There my Mother clasps
Me. Let me be !
Feel o' the red earth !
Devon to me !

THE CLIFF CHURCH

HERE stand I,
Buttressed over the sea !
Time and sky
Take no toll from me.

To me, grey—
Wind-grey, flung with foam—
Ye that stray
Wild-foot, come ye home !

Mother, I—
Mother I will be !
Ere ye die,
Hear ! O sons at sea !

Shall I fall—
Leave my flock of graves?
Not for all
Your rebelling waves !

I stand fast—
Let the waters cry !
Here I last
To Eternity !

COUNTING THE STARS

THE cuckoo bird has long gone home
And owls instead and flitting jars
Call out, call out for us to come,
My Love and me, to count the stars;
And into this wide orchard rove—
The whispering trees scarce give us room,
They drop their petals on my Love
And me beneath the apple bloom.

And each pale petal is alive
With dew of twilight from the sky,
Where all the stars hang in their hive—
Such scores to count, my Love and I!
The boughs below, the boughs above,
We scatter, lest their twisted gloom
Should stay the counting of my Love
And me beneath the apple bloom.

And when the Mother Moon comes by
And puts the little stars to bed,
We count, my timid Love and I,
The pretty apple stars instead;
Until at last all lights remove,
And dark sleep, dropping on the combe,
Fastens the eyelids of my Love
And me beneath the apple bloom.

THE MOOR GRAVE

I LIE out here under a heather sod,
A moor-stone at my head; the moor winds play above.
I lie out here. . . . The graveyard of their God
Was not for desperate me who died for love !
I lie out here under the sun and moon;
Across me ponies stride, and curlews cry.
I have no tombstone screed—no: "Soon
To glory shall she rise !" But peace have I !

THE COVE

HERE the waves a refuge find,
Hunted rain, and sobbing wind,
And darling sun.
To the velvet-thatchèd homes
Soft the sea-song silence comes
When day is done.

Here's the safeguard of each hill,
And the telling of the rill
To its dear sea.
Home to rest, the south wind brings
Ever drifted mutterings
Of tyranny.

Ships, like drunken sailors, reel,
Ships, like silver shadows, steal
Along the sky.
Rocks are green with wind-blown things,
Seaweeds furl their feathered rings,
And seabirds cry.

Corner true! thou shyest gem,
Clinging to the jealous hem
Of weary earth!
Heart's delight shall never fail,
So thou keep thy hidden tale
Of grief and mirth!

MOUNTAIN LOVERS

THE dawn's pale finger from her eyes
Is brushing out the cobweb sleep;
See how the crimson clothes the sky,
And out of dark the mountains leap!
Now guides and hunters strap their gears,
The birds peep out, the mice run in;
A snow-wind moves the nose to tears,
And flowers to open just begin.

    Then hand in hand with Lover Hope
    The strong-eyed, with our feet a-swing
    We'll go a-marching up the slope
    Of Young Enchantment's promising.

And now the clock is set at noon;
The butterflies are kittens black;
And cowbells tumble out a tune
Which yellow bees do mumble back.
We've climbed the snow into the sky;
Below, streams run a tinkling race,
And valleys glisten drowsily,
For all the world lies on its face.

The crystals bubble from the pine,
And grasses teem with little legs—

    Then drink the cup of Lover Joy,
    Who, silver-naked, goes about;
    Till eager heart has got its cloy
    Of wine that chases trouble out.

Now Sun has mellowed out the day,
The shadows play us hide and seek.
The cricket's legs have had their say;
And burned is every traveller's cheek.
Blueberries are ripe and warm,
Sparkle-fairies swim to land;
Hay is packing to the farm,
Cows, for milkmaids begging, stand.
Flaky trouts smoke in the dish,
Amber brews invite the throat—

    Then let full Plenty's droning song
    Play harvest music to your ear,
    Brave Lover Rest has come along
    To drug the senses of his dear.

Dew is blessing all the air,
Steel-bright stars are winking points,
Hush is fallen, eyelids stare,

Rheum comes crackling at the joints.
Wood-smoke tingles in the nose,
Moon goes flying like a sail,
Frost is nipping at the toes,
Drowsy drags the evening tale.
Windy clouds like flighting geese
Mountain-mad the heavens haunt—

Then take the kiss of Lover Sleep,
Who slyly steals the light of eyes—
Let monk, and maid, and martyr, keep
Their vigils, chant their threnodies!

HIGHLAND SPRING

THERE's mating madness in the air,
Passionate, grave! The blossoms burst;
The burns run quick to lips a-thirst;
And solemn gaze young maids, heart-free.

The white clouds race, the sun rays flare
And turn to gold the pallid mist;
With greedy mouth the Spring has kissed
The wind that links the sky with sea.

The blue and lonely mountains stare,
As if to draw the blue above.
The hour is come! O Flower of Love!
I can no longer keep from thee!

THE DOWNS

O THE Down high to the cool sky;
And the feel of the sun-warmed moss!
And each cardoon, like a full moon
Fairy-spun of the thistle floss;
And the beech-grove, and a wood-dove,
And the trail where the shepherds pass;
And the lark's song, and the wind-song,
And the scent of the parching grass!

ON A SOLDIER'S FUNERAL

No pipes have skirled;
But Heaven's wildest music blares;
Above the compound lightning flares,
The rain is whirled.

No drums shall roll—
Only a private soldier gone!
The cold light paints no funeral stone—
No bell need toll!

He lived his tame
And little day of silent tasks
And silent duty—no one asks
To know his name.

The milestones fade
Along the road that he has come.
No cheer of music takes him home—
His wage is paid.

The wind shrills high,
The darkened day is chasing grief
With lash of blinding rain—and brief
The footfalls die.

OLD YEAR

Tonight Old Year must die,
And join the vagabonding shades of time,
And haunt, and sob, and sigh
Around the tower where soon New Year will chime.

How fast the slim feet move!
The fiddles whine, the warbling oboes toot,
Lips whisper, eyes look love—
And Old Year's dying, dying underfoot!

So mute and spent, so wan—
Poor corse—beneath the laughter flying by;
The revel dances on
And treads you to the dust—condemned to die!

The moonlight floods the grass,
The music's hushed, and all the festal din;
The pale musicians pass,
Each clasping close his green-cased violin.

Old Year !—not breathing now,
Along the polished floor you lie alone;
I bend, and touch your brow—
The dead year, that has slipped away and gone !

WIND, WIND!

WIND, wind—heather gipsy,
Whistling in my tree!
All the heart of me is tipsy
On the sound of thee!
Sweet with scent of clover,
Salt with breath of sea.
Wind, wind—wayman lover,
Whistling in my tree!

STREET LAMPS

Lamps, lamps! Lamps ev'rywhere!
You wistful, gay, and burning eyes,
You stars low-driven from the skies
Down on the rainy air.

You merchant eyes, that never tire
Of spying out our little ways;
Of summing up our little days
In ledgerings of fire—

Inscrutable your nightly glance,
Your lighting and your snuffing out,
Your flicker through the windy rout,
Guiding this mazy dance.

O watchful, troubled gaze of gold,
Protecting us upon our beats—
You piteous glamour of the streets,
Youthless—and never old!

STRAW IN THE STREET

STRAW in the street!
My heart, oh! hearken—
Fate thrums its song of sorrow!
The windows darken. . . .
O God of all tomorrow!

Straw in the street!
To wintry sleeping
Turns all our summer laughter.
The brooms are sweeping. . . .
There's naught for me hereafter!

RHYME AFTER RAIN

STARRY-EYED is April morn,
Rainbells glitter on the thorn.
Birds are tuning down the lane
Patter song of fallen rain.
Spring can grieve, but Spring can be
Very life of minstrelsy!
   Gather the sob, gather the song!
   Neither will last, neither will last!
   All is yours, but not for long,
   Life travels fast!

Rainbow's dipping out to sea,
Lambs are whisp'ring devilry.
Leaves are sweet as e'er you've seen,
Sun is golden, grass is green.
Meadow's pied with flowers wet,
Thrushes sing: "Forget, forget!"
   Gather the grey, gather the gleam!
   Neither will last, neither will last!
   Certainty—'tis but a dream!
   Life travels fast!

Gorse has lit his lanterns all,
Cobwebbed thrift's a fairy ball,
Earth it smells as good as new,
Winds are merry, sky is blue.
Spring has laughter, Spring has tears,
Life has courage, life has fears.
    Gather the tears, gather the mirth!
    Neither will last, neither will last!
    Old Year's death is Young Year's birth—
    Life travels fast!

LET

My love lived there ! And now
'Tis but a shell of brick,
New-painted, flowered about—
So far from being quick
As night when stars die out.

From windows gaily wide,
Where once the curtained dark
My heaven used to hide,
The memories wan and stark
Troop down to me outside.

LOVE'S A FLOWER

Love's a flower, 'tis born and broken,
Plucked apace, and hugged apart;
Evening comes, it clings—poor token—
Dead and dry, on lover's heart.

Love's the rhyme of a summer minute
Woven close like hum of flies;
Sob of wind, and meaning in it
Dies away, as summer dies.

Love's a shimmery morning bubble
Puffed all gay from pipe of noon;
Spun aloft on breath of trouble—
Bursts in air—is gone—too soon!

ROSE AND YEW

Love flew by ! Young wedding day,
Peeping through her veil of dew,
Saw him, and her heart went fey—
His wings no shadows threw.

Love flew by ! Young day was gone,
Owls were hooting—Whoo-to-whoo !
Happy wedded lay alone,
Who'd vowed that love was true.

Love flies by, and drops a rose—
Drops a rose, a sprig of yew !
Happy these—but ah ! for those
Whose love has cried : Adieu !

MAGPIE

Magpie, lonely flying—
What do you bring to me?
Two for joy, and one for sorrow!
Loved today—is lost tomorrow!
Magpie! flying, flying—
What have you brought to me?

THE MOON AT DAWN

WHEN, at the dawn, the homeless breeze
Creeps back to wake the sleeping trees,
The moon steals down and no one sees!

Yes! in the morn, no watcher there,
She turns a face, once angel fair,
And smiles as only wantons dare!

. . . . . .

I saw her once, th' insatiate moon
Go stealing, coiffed in orange hood,
From Night, her lover, still in swoon—
All wicked she, who once was good!

RHYME OF THE LAND AND SEA

By the side of me—the immortal Pan—
Lies the sweetest thing of the sea;
In her gown of brine,
With her breast to mine,
And her drowned dark hair lies she!

But her smile—like the wine-red, shadowy sea,
When the day slides on and down—
By the gods, it is tender death to me!
In its waters dark I drown!
   "O slave of mine! Thou mystery
   Of smiling depths—I drown!"

PAST

THE clocks are chiming in my heart
A cobweb chime;
Old murmurings of days that die,
The sob of things a-drifting by.
The clocks are chiming in my heart!

The stars have twinkled, and died out—
Fair candles blown!
The hot desires burn low, and gone
To ash the fire that flamed anon.
The stars have twinkled, and died out!

Old journeys travel in my head!
They come and go—
Forgotten smiles of stranger friends,
Sweet weary miles and sweeter ends.
Old journeys travel in my head!

The leaves are dropping from my tree!
Dead leaves and flown,
The vine-leaf ghosts are round my brow,
For ever frosts and winter now.
The leaves are dropping from my tree!

48

THE GOLDEN GIPSY

(Lyric from 'The Little Dream')

THE windy hours through darkness fly—
Canst hear them, little heart?
New loves are born, and old loves die,
And kissing lips must part !
The dusky bees of passing years—
Canst see them, soul of mine?
From flower and flower supping tears
And pale sweet honey wine?

O flame that treads the marsh of time,
Flitting for ever low,
Where, through the black enchanted slime
We, desperate, following go—
Untimely fire ! we bid thee stay !
Into dark air above
The golden gipsy thins away . . .
    So has it been with love !

MOUNTAIN AIR

TELL me of Progress if you will,
But give me sunshine on a hill—
The grey rocks spiring to the blue,
The scent of larches, pinks, and dew,
And summer sighing in the trees,
And snowy breath on every breeze.
    Take towns and all that you'll find there,
    And leave me sun and mountain air!

TITTLE–TATTLE

Tittle-tattle! Scandal and japes,
Gibe, and gossip, and folly's rattle!
Ringed to fashion, caught like apes
In your cage of tittle-tattle!

Mean your skies,
And mean the ways you tread;
The meanness of your eyes
Is never fully fed.
You that have birth
In gold and grovellings!
You superfluity
Of miserable earth,
You trousered things
And women without souls—
Out of the sunlight
To your holes!

Tittle-tattle! Whisper and pry!
Sneers and snigger, and empty prattle!
Truth and charity into a lie
To the tune of tittle-tattle!

THE FLOWER

THERE's a flower, with a cup—
A cup of dew;
Golden god plucked it up
And gave it you.

If you shake—let it spill—
Its pretty rain,
All the world will not fill
It up again.

Careless death it must die,
And, like a weed,
In the sun ever lie
Disherited.

VOICE IN THE NIGHT

VOICE in the night—crying—
Down in the old sleeping Spanish city,
Darkened under her white stars;

What says the voice—its clear lingering anguish?
　Just the watchman telling his dateless tale of safety?
　Just a roadman flinging to the moon his song?
No! 'Tis one deprived—a lover's prayer for pity,
　Just his cry: "How long!"

AVOWAL

Thou art my Love, and I alway,
That nothing rueful thee dismay,
My every waking thought intend
From this beginning to the end,
And in my sleep I dream of thee
That unto me thou linkèd art,
And we are sailing, thou and I,
To watch the silver fishes fly,
The stars uncounted in the sky,
And that great floorway of the sea.
Then come with me if thou wouldst know
A summer that will never go,
Flowers unfading and the tune
Of sheepbells wandering in June.
And I will conjure till these seem
Such part of elfin land to thee,
That backed on swallow thou shalt fly
And chase the thistle floating by,
And ride on moonbeams through the sky
To rob dark night of ecstasy.

I am a world devoted quite,
That lives but when thou'rt in my sight,
Ah ! dwell in me, and I will try
To make thee happy till I die !

IN WAR TIME

VALLEY OF THE SHADOW

God, I am travelling out to death's sea,
   I, who exulted in sunshine and laughter,
Dreamed not of dying—death is such waste of me!—
   Grant me one prayer: Doom not the hereafter
Of mankind to war, as though I had died not—
   I, who in battle, my comrade's arm linking,
Shouted and sang, life in my pulses hot
   Throbbing and dancing! Let not my sinking
In dark be for naught, my death a vain thing!
   God, let me know it the end of man's fever!
Make my last breath a bugle call, carrying
   Peace o'er the valleys and cold hills for ever!

THE BELLS OF PEACE

LILIES are here, tall in the garden bed,
   And on the moor are still the buds of May;
Roses are here—and, tolling for our dead
   The Bells of Peace make summer holiday.

And do *they* hear, who in their Springtime went?
   The young, the brave young, leaving all behind,
All of their fate, love, laughter, and content,
   The village sweetness and the western wind.

Leaving the quiet trees and the cattle red,
   The southern soft mist over granite tor—
Whispered from home, by secret valour led
   To face the horror that their souls abhor.

Here in the starlight to the owl's "To-whoo!"
   They wandered once, they wander still, maybe,
Dreaming of home, clinging the long night thro'
   To sound and sight fastened in memory.

Here in the sunlight and the bracken green—
    Wild happy roses starring every lane—
Eager to reach the good that might have been,
    They were at peace. Are they at peace again?

Bells of remembrance, on this summer's eve
    Of our relief, Peace and Goodwill ring in !
Ring out the Past, and let not Hate bereave
    Our dreaming Dead of all they died to win !

PICARDY

When the trees blossom again;
  When our spirits lighten—
When in quick sun and rain
  Once more the green fields brighten;
Each golden flower those fields among,
The hum of thrifting bee,
Will be the risen flower and song
Of Youth's mortality.

When the birds flutter their wings,
  When our scars are healing—
When the furry-footed things
  At night again are stealing;
Then through the wheat each rippling wave,
The fragrance of flower breath
Will bring a message from the grave,
A whispering from death.

When the sweet waters can flow;
   When the world's forgetting—
When once more the cattle low
   At golden calm sun-setting;
Each peaceful evening's murmur, then,
And sigh the waters give,
Will tell immortal tale of men
Who died that we might live.

YOUTH'S OWN

Out of the fields I see them pass,
    Youth's own battalion—
Like moonlight ghosting over grass,
    To dark oblivion.

They have a wintry march to go—
    Bugle and fife and drum !
With music softer than the snow-
    Fall, flurrying, they come !

They have a solemn tryst to keep
    Out on the starry heath;
To fling them down, and sleep and sleep
    Beyond Reveille—Death !

Since Youth has vanished from our eyes,
    Who of us glad can be?
Who will be grieving, when he dies
    And leaves this Calvary?

WONDER

If God is thrilled by a battle cry,
    If He can bless the moaning fight,
If when the trampling charge goes by
    God himself is the leading knight;
If God laughs when the guns thunder,
    If He yells when the bullet sings—
Then, bewildered, I but wonder
    God of Love can love such things!

.   .   .   .   .   .

The white gulls wheeling over the plough,
    The sun, the reddening trees—
We being enemies, I and thou,
    There is no meaning in these.
There is no flight on the wings of Spring,
    No scent in the summer rose,
The roundelays that the blackbirds sing—
    There is no meaning in those!

If you must kill me—why the lark,
   The hawthorn bud, and the corn?
Why do the stars bedew the dark?
   Why is the blossom born?
If I must kill you—why the kiss
   Which made you? There is no why!
If it be true we were born for this—
   Merciless God, goodbye!

UNKNOWN

You who had worked in perfect ways
To turn the wheel of nights and days,
Who coaxed to life each running rill
And froze the snow-crown on the hill,
The cold, the starry flocks who drove,
And made the circling seasons move;
How came your jesting purpose when
You fashioned monkeys into men?

You who invented peacock's dress—
You, Lord of cruel happiness!—
Who improvised all flight and song
And loved and killed the whole day long,
And filled with colour to the brim
The cup of your completed whim!
What set you frolicking when we
Were given power to feel and see?

Why not have kept the stellar plan
Quite soulless and absolved from man?
What heavy need to make this thing—
A monkey with an angel's wing;

A murderous poor saint who reaps
His fields of death, and, seeing—weeps!
No!—if the saffron day could sigh
And sway unconscious—Why am I?

. . . . . .

Unknown! You slept one afternoon
And dreamed, and turned, and woke too soon!
The sorrel glowed, and the bees hummed,
And Mother Nature's fingers strummed,
And flock of dandelion was blown,
And the yew-trees cast their shadows down;
Such beauty seemed to you forlorn—
And lo!—this playboy, Man, was born!

THE PRAYER

If on a Spring night I went by
And God were standing there,
What is the prayer that I would cry
To Him? This is the prayer:
   O Lord of Courage grave,
   O Master of this night of Spring!
   Make firm in me a heart too brave
   To ask Thee anything!

I ASK

My happy lime is gold with flowers;
From noon to noon the breezes blow
Their love pipes; and the wild bees beat
Their drums, and sack the blossom bowers. . . .
Yet, stifling in the valley heat
A woman's dying there below!

Between the blowing rose so red
And honey-saffroned lily cup,
Receiving heaven, so I lie. . . .
But down the field a calf lies dead;
At this same burning summer sky
Its velvet darkened eye looks up.

.   .   .   .   .   .

Behind the fairest masks of life
Dwells ever that pale constant death.
Philosophers! What shall we say?
Must we keep wistful death to wife?
Or hide her image quite away,
And, wanton, draw forgetful breath?

TIME

BENEATH this vast serene of sky
Where worlds are but as mica dust,
From age to age the wind goes by;
Unnumbered summer burns the grass.
On granite rocks, at rest from strife,
The æons lie in lichen rust.
Then what is man's so brittle life?—
The humming of the bees that pass!

FRIVOLS

MR. COLUMMY

MR. COLUMMY is out in his park,
   He and his tummy,
   Mr. Colummy.
As soon as they see him the little dogs bark;
   Oh! ever so rummy
   Is Mr. Colummy.

Mr. Colummy has riz' with the lark;
   Beginnings were slummy
   With Mr. Colummy.
He once was a minnow, and now he's a shark.
   He used to say: 'Lumme!'
   Did Mr. Colummy.

Mrs. Colummy is pretty and dark,
   Awfully plummy
   Mrs. Colummy!
Her parents belonged to the island of Sark.
   She's not very chummy
   With Mr. Colummy.

Master Colummy—his cares do not cark !—
   That fat little dummy
   Takes after his mummy.
There's never quite anything up to his mark;
   Life's almost too crummy
   For Master Colummy !

MAYDAY ON DARTMOOR

MAYDAY wears a summer smile,
Mayday is a mummer
Sleepy rills and fat green fields—
All the coat of summer.
Sturdy blackthorn twining stars,
Golden gorse a-shining,
All the tors blow honey-sweet
Honey deaths to pining!

Cuckoo's tell-a-secret song
Mocks the bells, mocks the bells;
Whistle back and win along!
Win along, and follow!
Cuckoo's on the restless moor,
Church is in the hollow!

Moorland birdies hopping by,
Skylark's dew a-dropping;
Whispers from the valley stream,
Crisp the ponies' cropping!

Clash the bells ! Old church—have done
Of wishing you may get me !
I'll go worshipping the sun
While the sun will let me !

Cuckoo's fetter-breaking song
Mocks the bells, mocks the bells !
Come, my heart ! Let's go along !
Go along, and follow !
Cuckoo's on the living moor,
Church is in the hollow !

HOLIDAY SONG

Here's a day of cap and bells!
Cows shake out a silver dinning;
Shed your virtues, come a-sinning,
Leave your morals to their cells!

Birds are piping, insects hum;
Take the path of play and laughter!
Why go caring what comes after?
Nature's drum-sticks all a-drum!

Clowns and Christians count the loss!
Ope your mouth—let berries tumble!
Eat no more of pie that's humble!
Let your heart play pitch and toss!

When the cup of joy grows stale
Bunnies all shall cease their funning,
Sunflowers have enough of sunning,
Cats look tired, and kittens pale!

DEDICATIONS TO TWO GODSONS

I

SMALL Friend, when your infatuate sire
Conferred on you the name of John,
And to myself expressed desire
That skyward I should lead you on;
How little did he know of me—
Of you, my godkin, even less—
But we conspirators must be
And hide up our unworthiness.

Together we will tread the way
That leads to mansions in the sky,
Or, if we don't, at least we'll say
We surely mean to, by and by.
And while we stay on solid earth
And still postpone our holy ends,
We'll inch by inch increase our girth,
And be, I hope, the best of friends.

II

SMALL John, I fear when you grow up you'll say:
"They gave to me as pilot to the sky
A silly man who didn't know the way,
And couldn't put me wise—I wonder why?
He never gave me book morocco-bound
Or silver cup with christening date engraved;
He let me wander round and round and round,
And quite neglected for to get me saved!"

Well, little John, I freely do confess
That I'm no guide towards the better Land,
But, if in this, our earthly wilderness,
You falter, and should need a helping hand—
Then here it is, perhaps not over-clean,
And dabbled rather deep in ink and that—
But willing; and at all events, I mean
You shall have nothing else to wonder at.

UNICORNS

If I were asked to take my pick
Of all the creatures fantastic,
Gryphons and phœnixes and such,
Dragons and dolphins, and the much
Reported serpent of the sea,
Vampires, whichever they may be,
March hares, mad rabbits, or the Sphinx,
Or all the many missing links—
                    Well!
There's something to be said for fauns—
But I should choose white unicorns!

IN A VOLUME OF 27 PLAYS (J. G.)

SOLD ON BEHALF OF A HOSPITAL

THE buyer gapes and stammers: "What!
You mean to tell me I have got
To read these Plays—to read them all!
Oh! no—the man's a criminal,
With twenty-seven mortal sins!—
Ye little fishes and your fins!
Too hot! It comforts me to think
They must have driven him to drink!"

Ah! yes, they did; and that is why
I make the buyer this reply:
"Far better burned than read, poor buyer;
So spare your eyes, and feed your fire!"

IN A COPY OF 'FOUR FORSYTE STORIES'

SOLD ON BEHALF OF A HOUSING SCHEME

STROPHE:

"AN author who has what is called a vogue—
That can, like mushroom, spring up overnight—
A thing of air, and apt to vanish quite—
Runs ev'ry risk that he may seem a rogue
When signed editions he goes marketing,
Priced at as many guineas as he dare,
And, trusting to the Public's want of flair,
Makes major money from a minor thing."

ANTISTROPHE:

"BUT, carping Sir, your author is a bird
Who, like as not, believes that he will sing
And soar, until the booklet signed, will bring
A price that makes its present price absurd.
A very peacock-fantail-phœnix, he;
The more you warn him of his coming fall
Or tell him that he's nothing worth at all,
The more his pinnacle in air he'll see!"

TO PRINCETON

FROM A WEARY WAYFARER

Lord! I plump for Princeton—
Peaceful there I be!
Peace and plump and Princeton
All begin with P!

ON ACCIDENTAL EXCHANGE OF HATS
(OPERA)

WITH JOHN MASEFIELD

O FRIENDLY hat—hat of my friend !
And must I pack thee up and end
That brief encircling halo torn
From noble Masefield's peg, and worn
In ecstasy one hour ! Dear hat !
So much more beautiful than that
I left behind—from me depart !
Be crushed once more against *his* heart !

FOR LOVE OF BEASTS

PRAYER FOR GENTLENESS TO ALL CREATURES

To all the humble beasts there be,
To all the birds on land and sea,
Great Spirit! sweet protection give,
That free and happy they may live!

And to our hearts the rapture bring
Of love for every living thing;
Make of us all one kin, and bless
Our ways with Christ's own gentleness!

TO MY DOG

My dear! When I leave you
I always drop a bit of me—
A holy glove or sainted shoe—
Your wistful corse I leave it to,
For all your soul has followed me—
How could I have the stony heart
So to abandon you!

My dear! When you leave me
You drop no glove, no sainted shoe;
And yet you know what humans be—
Mere blocks of dull monstrosity!
My spirit cannot follow you
When you're away, with all its heart
As yours can follow me.

My dear! Since we must leave
(One sorry day) I you, you me;
I'll learn your wistful way to grieve;
Then through the ages we'll retrieve
Each other's scent and company;
And longing shall not pull my heart—
As now you pull my sleeve!

LOST

In the grey wilderness—a dog!
Where are his friends—the scents he knew?
Who owned him, fed him, as he grew
From pup to shadow lost in fog?

His little world has thinned away;
He runs—a phantom; Fate will drive
Him up street, down street, all the day
And then at night no shelter give.

The trail is vapoured, gone the sense
Of human refuge; run and run,
'Tis all he can, not knowing where
Or whither—run, and sniff, and shun!

In the grey wilderness—a ghost,
A thin brown helpless ghost astray!
Can no one stay him, show the way
To home? Chase out that look: 'I'm lost!'

DONKEYS

When to God's Fondouk the donkeys are taken—
  Donkeys of Barbary, Sicily, Spain—
If peradventure the Deity waken
  He shall not easily slumber again.

Where in the sweet of the straw they have laid them,
  Broken and dead of their burdens and sores,
He, for a change, shall remember He made them—
  One of the best of His numerous chores.

Order from someone a sigh of repentance—
  Donkeys of Syria, Araby, Greece—
Over the Fondouk distemper the sentence:
  "For God's own forsaken—the Stable of Peace!"

NEVER GET OUT!

I KNEW a little Serval cat—
      Never get out!
Would pad all day from this to that—
      Never get out!
From bar to bar she'd turn and turn,
And in her eyes a fire would burn—
(From her Zoölogy we learn!)
      Never get out!

But if by hap a ray of sun
Came shining in her cage, she'd run
And sit upon her haunches where
Into the open she could stare
And with the free that sunlight share—
      Never get out!

That catling's jungle heart forlorn
Will die as wild as it was born. . . .
If I could cage the human race
Awhile like her, in prisoned space,
And teach them what it is to face
      Never get out!

PITIFUL

WHEN God made man to live his hour,
   And hitch his wagon to a star,
He made a being without power
   To see His creatures as they are.
He made a masterpiece of will,
   Superb above its mortal lot,
Invincible by any ill . . .
   Imagination He forgot!

This man of God, with every wish
   To earn the joy of Kingdom Come,
Will prison up the golden fish
   In bowl no bigger than a drum.
And though he'll wither from remorse
   When he refuses Duty's call,
He'll cut the tail off every horse
   And carve each helpless animal.

No spur to humour doth he want,
   In wit the earth he overlords,
Yet drives the hapless elephant
   To clown and tumble on "the boards."

This man, of every learning chief,
   So wise that he can read the skies,
Can fail to read the wordless grief
   That haunts a prisoned monkey's eyes.

He'll prate of "Mercy to the weak,"
   And strive to lengthen human breath,
But starve the little gaping beak,
   And hunt the timid hare to death.
Though, with a spirit wild as wind
   The world at liberty he'd see,
He cannot any reason find
   To set the tameless tiger free.

Such healing victories he wins,
   And drugs away the mother's pangs,
But sets his god-forsaken 'gins'
   To mangle rabbits with their fangs.
Devote, he'd travel all the roads
   To track and vanquish all the pains,
And yet—the wagon overloads,
   The watch-dog to his barrel chains.

He'll soar the heavens in his flight,
   To measure Nature's majesty;
Yet take his children to delight
   In captive eagle's tragedy.

This man, in knowledge absolute,
   Who right and love and honour woos,
Yet keeps the pitiful poor brute
   To mope and languish in his Zoos.

     You creatures wild, of field and air,
        Keep far from men, where'er they go!
     God set no speculation there—
        Alack! We know not what we do!

AKIN

Who that has marked the white owl's flight
   Or blessed the lark at noon,
Or listened of a summer night
   And startled at the loon.
Who that has browsed with blunt-nosed sheep
   Or spied an adder drink,
Or seen a baby skunk asleep,
   Or heard the bob-o-link—

Who so has fared, and felt no free
   Delight within him run;
Then of the great freemasonry
   Be sure he is not one.
But if his sentient ardour flow
   For things that pad or fly,
With you and me—oh ! surely know
   He hath affinity.

     .   .   .   .   .

America and England breed
   Those who are brothers still,
For that the beasts they love; and heed
   Bird music on the hill !

IMPRESSIONS

SILVER POINT

Sharp against a sky of grey
Pigeon's nest in naked tree;
Every silver twig up-curled,
Not a budding leaf unfurled,
Not a breath to fan the day !

World aspiring and severe,
Not a hum of fly or bee,
Not a song and not a cry,
Not a perfume stealing by—
Stillest moment of the year !

BOTTICELLI'S 'THE BIRTH OF VENUS'

THE Spring wind fans her hair,
And after her fly little waves,
Her feet are shod in pearly shoon,
And down her foam-white breast do shine
Petals encarnadine.

Her eyes are deaths to care,
Her eyes of love are tender caves.
The blossoms blowing on the trees—
The leafy Spring's enchanted stir—
The humming of the golden bees—
All are the voice of her!

BOTTICELLI'S 'PRIMAVERA'

HANDMAIDS of the Queen of Love!
Earth grows white with stars;
Young Fertility is leaping,
Soft the springing grasses teem;
Slothful days have left their sleeping—
You alone do dream!

Maidens of the Queen of Flowers!
Trees hang orange lamps;
All the winds are pollen blowing;
Through the failing golden light
Gentle Gravity is going—
Passion is the Night!

Maidens of the silver feet!
Violent Spring's awake!
Hearts are seeking, birds are nesting;
Earth below and skies above
Teach the hour of sweet unresting!—
All the world is Love!

THE CUP

Here is my Cup;
A crystal well,
Where the wind's rough fluting dies
To the thin-tuned sigh of a shell!
The very breath
Of melody,
In sob and song
She's singing me!

Here is my Cup;
A fairy soul,
With the sun all gold on her curves,
And the moon milk-white in her bowl!
As twilight dark,
Like dew a-shine,
The goblet she
Of ev'ry wine.

AUTUMN BY THE SEA

WE'LL hear the uncompanioned murmur of the swell,
And touch the driftwood, delicately grey,
And with our quickened senses smell
The sea-flowers all the day.

We'll count the white gulls pasturing on meadows
brown,
And gaze into the arches of the blue,
Till evening's ice comes stealing down
From those far fields of dew.

Now slow the crimson sun-god swathes his eye, and
sails
To sleep in his innumerable cloak;
And gentle heat's gold pathway fails
In autumn's opal smoke·

Then long we'll watch the journey of the soft half-
moon—
A gold-bright moth slow-spinning up the sky,
And know the dark flight—all too soon—
Of land-birds wheeling by.

Through all the black wide night of stars our souls
    shall touch
The sky, in this long quietude of things,
And gain brief freedom from the clutch
Of life's encompassings.

PROMENADE

ALL sweet and startled gravity,
My Love comes walking from the Park;
Her eyes are full of what they've seen—
The little bushes puffing green,
The candles pale that light the chestnut-tree.

The tulip and the jonquil spies;
The sunshine and the sudden dark;
The dance of buds; and Madam Dove,
Sir Blackbird fluting to his Love—
These little loves my Love has in her eyes.

In dainty shoes and subtle hose
My Love comes walking from the Park;
She is, I swear, the sweetest thing
That ever left the heart of Spring,
To tell the secret: Whence the pollen blows!

THE FRANCE FLOWER

I STROLL forth this flowery day
Of "print frocks" and buds of may,
And speedwells of tender blue
Whom no sky can match for hue.

I love well my English home;
Yet far thoughts do stealing come
To throng me like honey-bees,
Till far flowers my fancy sees—

'Tis almond against the snows,
And gentian, and mountain rose,
And iris, in purple bright,
The France flower, the flower of light!

SWEET OATH IN MALLORCA

IF you had, suddenly, been where I've been
Under the sun among the almond flowers,
If you had dreamed and seen what I have seen—
The old grey olives and the old grey towers;
If, in bewilderment, there had come to you
Over the hills, beneath the evening star,
The tinkling of the sheepbells, or the blue
Gleaming from where the happy wild flowers are;
If you'd been wafted to that fairy-land,
And in delight been lost and lost again,
And walking with me waved a friendly hand
To children smiling with the eyes of Spain,
And in full day beheld the young moon fly—
Then had you sworn the same sweet oath as I!

AT VALDEMOSA: MALLORCA

(January 2, 1930)

LEMONS and roses—guide-book said—
A courtyard, and a simple bed
Or two, for that romantic pair!
And so it was, when I was there.

In quarters that were so confined
You may have found that lady's mind
A little trying, day by day;
And so you did—or so they say!

But with such wonders for your sight,
Such scatter of the stars at night,
Such sunset light upon the hills,
What need you reck of little ills?

You had a prospect to the sea
That certainly appealed to me,
The garden trim, the valley fair,
The folded hills, the limpid air,

The almond, winter-blossoming,
The buds not waiting for the Spring,
The olive trees, the tinkling bells
Of sheep among the asphodels.

What with the Paradise down there,
The scent of lemons on the air,
And all the music that you scored—
Chopin! I know you were not bored!

NOVEMBER

Leaves from the elm trees flying—
Summer to autumn flown—
Out on the lawn is lying
Mulberry's golden gown.

Never a bird is singing,
Never a plant has bloom,
Only the fantails winging
White on the windy gloom.

We can no more remember
Perfume of rose or hay;
Far from this dark November
Beauty has passed away.

Not till the Spring recapture
Joy as it flits along,
Shall we regain the rapture
Either of scent or song!

MERLE

THE sea and sky are grey—
    As with the grief of those who've mourned;
Yet through this drear December day
    A lonely merle to song has turned.

Brave bird, for you no fears !
    Though to the sun you're strange—as we,
Across the waste of these last years
    Bereft of all hilarity.

Then, bird ! be voice for all
    The sad who have forgotten song.
Shake far that trilling lift and fall
    Of notes, and take our hearts along !

DESERT SONG

As I came on from Santa Fé,
The desert road by night and day,
The desert wilds ran far and free
Beneath the wind of desert sea.

    But—ah ! my heart !—to know again
    The scent of rain, the scent of rain !

And I'd in fancy scale the air
Beyond those yellow mountains bare,
And so with dizzy bird survey
A thousand miles of shining day.
And I would glean the gold of sun
And mark his curving glory run
Its fiery course, and eager turn
My cheek and pallid brow to burn.

    But—oh ! my heart !—to feel again
    The wet of rain, the wet of rain !

And wakeful all the night I'd lie
And watch the dark infinity,
And count the stars that wheel and spin,
And drink the frosty æther in;
And I would hear the desert song
That silence sings the whole night long,
And day by day the whisper pass
Of parching heat through desert grass.

But—oh ! my heart !—to hear again
The drip of rain, the drip of rain !

When I rode on from Santa Fé,
That desert road by night and day,
There came at last a little sigh,
A puff of white across the sky.

And—ah ! my heart !—I knew again
The scent of rain, the scent of rain !

AT SUNSET

I've seen the moon, with lifted wing—
   A white hawk—over a cypress tree;
The lover's star, the bloom of Spring,
   And evening folded on Tennessee.

I've seen the little streams run down—
   All smoke-blue, lost in færie;
And far, the violet mountains crown
   The darkness breathing on Tennessee.

I've seen the Beautiful, so clear—
   And it has gone to the heart of me;
So there'll be magic ever near
   To me, remembering Tennessee.

THE PASS OF THE SONG

Lone and far, lone and far
On a track that is strange and long,
From the morning's rim to the evening star
To the Pass of the silent song.

Far and lone, far and lone,
Where the rise and the rocks are bare,
And the sun has flamed, and the moon has shone
On the æons of desert air.

Lone and far, lone and far,
Till the eye to the summit wins,
And below, the plains and the mountains are,
And the lilt of the song begins.

Far and lone, far and lone
Will the tune of it lift and wend,
In a silent song of a world unknown
And a dream that will never end.

AUTUMN

When every leaf has different hue
And flames of birch trees blow,
And high against November blue
The white cloud's bent in bow;

When buzzard hawk wheels in the sun,
And bracken crowns the Cleave,
And autumn stains the heather dun,
And wan buds make believe;

When droning thresher hums its song
And tale of harvest proves,
And rusty steers the lane-ways throng,
And grey birds flit in droves;

Then bird, and beast, and every tree
And those few flowers that blow,
Against the winter hearten me
Who would no winter know !

DREAM HOUSE

Down on our house good shelter falls
From those high neighbouring white walls,
And here it dreams among its flowers
And bushes bright with summer showers.

Its creepered brick soaks up the smile
Of noon and afternoon, the while
The bees go tunnelling the deep
Dim lily bells that sway and sleep.

The day slips on, and sun's hot eye
Cools in the lime trees, down the sky.
'Tis twilight now, the birds refrain
From song, and all is still again.

Now night creeps over, distance hides;
The white house—a tall iceberg—rides;
A chafer breaks the darkened swoon,
And white wide roses scan the moon.

FLOWERS

O MY flowers! On your bosom
Sweet and pale the silver-cradled
Night shall swoon away with love.

On your carpet gay, of blossom
Blue and gold, the softly-sandalled
Breeze shall dance from noon to noon.

O my flowers! At your coming
All the earth glows into gladness,
Dark and cloudy griefs remove.

In my heart the wind is roaming
Wild, the grass is parched with sadness.
Spring! my lovely Spring, come soon!

THE NATIVE STAR

I HAVE sailed South to a new light,
   New stars, and seen the Plough
Dip to the Cross, and watched the bright
   Fish spraying from the prow.
Lagoons and palmgroves I have spied,
   And loom of mangrove tree;
Yet craved for a salt heaven wide
   Above the English sea.

I have been far afoot among
   Old deserts and great hills,
And trailed across the forests long
   That feed the lumber mills.
At memory of smiling downs
   Those grander visions pass,
For well I know to me the crown's
   A day on English grass.

I have been mazed and mazed again
   Where California glows;
And marvelled at a flowered Spain—
   Her orange and her rose;

121

I've dreamed Japan, all cherry white;
    Yet would I liefer see
The Springtime stars of blossom light
    An English apple tree.

In many countries I have stood
    Where miracles have thronged
To God's imaginative mood,
    And yet my heart has longed
For English sound and scent and scene
    Though all my reason knows
They'll never be, have never been
    Fit to compare with those.

Why this should be I cannot tell,
    Of Man it seems decreed
That he shall feel the moving spell
    Of his especial breed.
Muezzin call to night and morn—
    "Brothers, or near or far,
Be not dismayed that each is born
    Under his native star !"

TO LIBERTY

Bird, my bird, unwearied flying
Over the sands, over the sea—
Bird of Light, thou soul undying!
God that is not, yet shall be!

Bird, my bird, with eyes of morning,
Under the snow, under the night—
On! thou starry spirit, scorning
Refuge for the wings of light!

Bird, my bird, the day is breaking,
Over the sands, over the sea—
Rose beneath the darkness, waking
Summer's immortality!

Bird, my bird, I hear thee singing,
Over the waste, over the foam,
Clear and high, the far white-winging
Song of Freedom, flighting home!

Bird, my bird, unwearied flying
Over the sands, over the sea—
Soul of Liberty, undying!
God that is not, yet shall be!

THE SUN, THE MOON, THE
ENDLESS DREAM

PRAISED BE THE SUN!

IF in a world where life is born of death,
And from the fate of dying none is free,
And the chief law is Strife, and ev'ry breath
Of man and beast and bird and fish and tree
Is daily drawn in dissolution's doubt—
If in a world like this there can be one
Among the rounding shows to single out
For praise—then will I praise the Sun!
The Sun, the Sun!—though it can deserts make,
And light its lanterns in their windswept bones;
I praise the Sun that doth with glory flake
The flowering meadows and the very stones;
That can the world transfigure to my eye,
And warm to substance all that shadows by.
    Praising I live, and when I foundered be,
    O thou belovèd Sunlight, cover me!

TO BEAUTY

Beauty on your wings—flying the far blue,
Flower of man's heart whom no God made;
Star, leaf-breath, and gliding shadow,
Fly with me, too, awhile!

Bring me knowledge:
How the pansies are made, and the cuckoo's song!
And the little owls, grey in the evening, three on a
     gate;
The goldcups a-field, the flight of the swallow:
The eyes of the cow who has calved;
The wind passing from ash-tree to ash-tree!

For thee shall I never cease aching?
Do the gnats ache that dance in the sun?
Do the flowers ache, or the bees rifling their gold?
Is it I only who ache?
Beauty! Fulfil me! Cool the heart of my desire!

SPRING

Come out ! It's Spring !
The elm-trees ! See ! They're blossoming !
All crimson-painted. Here's a flower
Come open ! Now with ev'ry hour
There'll be fresh pollen for that bee—
Oho ! No longer sleepy, he !

What song ! What song
Those greening hedges breaks along !
God ! There's performed in everything
A miracle of throat and wing.
Needs but a swallow to flit by
And print its pattern on the sky.

Oh ! Smell this air !
The wind it wanders ; everywhere
It plucks a scent. Ah ! Exquisite
The ache of Spring that comes with it !
And whence it comes, or where it goes,
The troubling wind of Spring—who knows ?

All now is still !
The sunlight's level on the hill.
There goes a furry groundling. Run !
You Spring-created rascal, run !
And—hark ! The blackbird's evening shout—
"The Spring ! The Spring ! Come out ! Come out !"

PEACE IN THE WORLD

(Message for the Livre d'Or de la Paix, Geneva)

GOD send us wit to banish far
The incense and the reeking breath,
The lances and the fame of war,
And all the devilments of death.
Let there be wisdom and increase,
The harvest reconcilement brings,
So shall we see the eyes of Peace,
And feel the wafting of Her wings.

BURY HILL

To this green hill a something dream-like clings,
Where day by day the little blunt sheep graze,
Threading the tussocks and the toadstool rings,
Nosing the barrows of the olden days.
An air drifts here that's sweet of sea and grass,
And down the combe-side living colour glows;
Spring, Summer, Fall, the chasing seasons pass
To Winter, even lovelier than those.

The dream is deep today, when all that's far
Of wandering water and of darkling wood,
Of weald and ghost-like Down combinèd are
In haze below this hill where God has stood.

Here I, too, stand until the light is gone,
And feed my wonder, while the sheep graze on.

SO MIGHT IT BE!

DEATH, when you come to me, tread with a footstep
   Light as the moon's on the grasses asleep,
So that I know not the moment of darkness,
   Know not the drag and the draw of the deep.

Death, when you come to me, let there be sunlight,
   Dogs and dear creatures about me at play,
Flowers in the fields and the song of the blackbird—
   Spring in the world when you fetch me away !

THE MOMENT WAITING

FOLDED is ev'ry sheep, the sunlight's gone,
A lonely bird re-takes its evening flight;
Warmth on the downs, and colour, there is none,
And yet, a Presence—in this lingered light
Conjured of sky and the green-coated chalk,
Of air no longer sunlit and so still—
Native and thin-embodied seems to walk,
As if devotional, upon this hill.

I could be fancying the ghosts of all
Who vivified these heights in olden days
Lurk in the void, and wait for dusk to fall
And cover them on their remembered ways.
There is a hushed suspense pervades this sweep
Of pallid grass, a spell unreal cast;
Even the fallen winds have feet that creep
Upon my sense, as if a spirit passed.

'Tis in a moment waiting, such as now,
When all is wan, away to the far sea,
We of the life ephemeral can bow

In recognition of eternity.
Sun and the moon and stars are sequestrate,
And time—it is not dawn nor noon nor night;
All is unbounded, and each mortal date
So little set as thistledown in flight.

MOON-NIGHT

THE moon shines full, the elm-trees stand
Like sentinels, and shadows spill,
And up that quiet, unearthly land
The sheepbells with their tinkling fill
A silence reaching to the sky;
The rounded farm-stacks that were gold
Now moonlit and unreal lie;
And all is magical and cold.

But here, beneath my window, one
Magnolia flower blooms, alight,
Moon-glinted, lovely, and alone,
As fastened in the hair of night,
And from it to my nostrils creep
Such spicy odours as might move
To raptured waking all who sleep,
The very moon herself, to love.

So may night breathe in beauty, when
My little flame blows out, and I
Back to the fold return, for then

It will be dream-like, and goodbye
Will not be harder than it must;
For life will leave me with a kiss
Upon my brow of moonlit dust—
If night be beautiful like this!

AMBERLEY WILDBROOKS

By this bright river bordering the mead
Beflagged by reed and rush and willow tree,
Where dragon-flies across the water lead
The wingèd rout of noonday revelry,
I stand ecstatic, silent, with a brain
Bemused, as stand bemused the tawny kine,
And hear high summer sink and lift again
And feel its spirit stealing into mine.

Here when in winter-time the wild brooks brimmed
And with their salty flood annulled the earth,
Till with a lake the dreaming Down was rimmed,
And wandering water-beauty came to birth
With floating birds, and the green icy sky,
And far the sun so pale and pitying shone;
Here on this bank, no less bemused, stood I
Until the winter's mood and mine were one.

Man is a dreamer, waking for a day,
Until the wild brooks of oblivion brim;
'Tis well his waking self should slip away,
And momentary dreaming comfort him;

For so he learns, before the long sleep comes,
That in himself revolves the starry scheme,
In him the winter's mute, the summer hums,
Just as it will be in the endless dream.